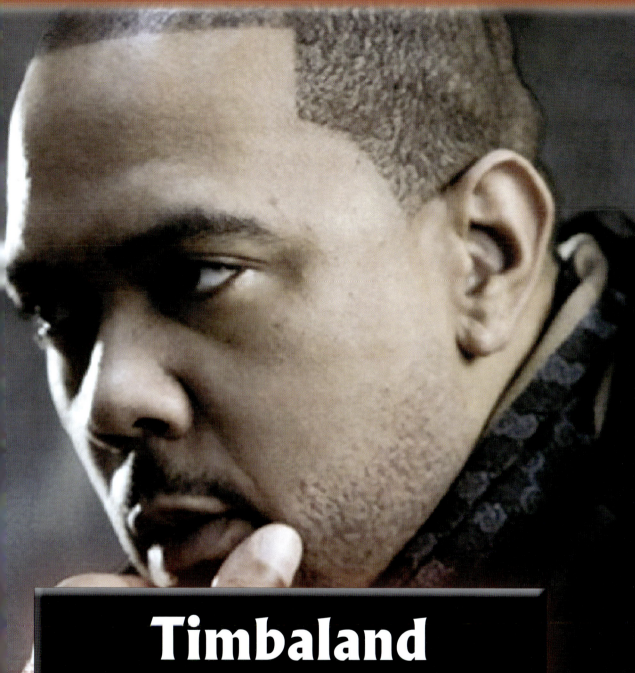

Timbaland

by C.F. Earl

Superstars of Hip-Hop

Alicia Keys

Beyoncé

Black Eyed Peas

Ciara

Dr. Dre

Drake

Eminem

50 Cent

Flo Rida

Hip Hop:
A Short History

Jay-Z

Kanye West

Lil Wayne

LL Cool J

Ludacris

Mary J. Blige

Notorious B.I.G.

Rihanna

Sean "Diddy" Combs

Snoop Dogg

T.I.

T-Pain

Timbaland

Tupac

Usher

Timbaland

by C.F. Earl

Mason Crest

Timbaland

Mason Crest
370 Reed Road
Broomall, Pennsylvania 19008
www.masoncrest.com

Printed and bound in the United States of America.

First printing
9 8 7 6 5 4 3 2 1

Library of Congress Cataloging-in-Publication Data

Earl, C.F.
  Timbaland / C.F. Earl.
    p. cm. – (Superstars of hip-hop)
  Includes index.
  ISBN 978-1-4222-2528-8 (hard cover) – ISBN 978-1-4222-2508-0 (series hardcover) – ISBN 978-1-4222-9230-3 (ebook)
  1. Timbaland (Musician)–Juvenile literature 2. Rap musicians–United States–Biography–Juvenile literature. I. Title.
  ML3930.T577E27 2012
  782.42164909–dc23
  [B]
                                2011020117

Produced by Harding House Publishing Services, Inc.
www.hardinghousepages.com
Interior Design by MK Bassett-Harvey.
Cover design by Torque Advertising & Design.

Publisher's notes:
• All quotations in this book come from original sources and contain the spelling and grammatical inconsistencies of the original text.
• The Web sites mentioned in this book were active at the time of publication. The publisher is not responsible for Web sites that have changed their addresses or discontinued operation since the date of publication. The publisher will review and update the Web site addresses each time the book is reprinted.

DISCLAIMER: The following story has been thoroughly researched, and to the best of our knowledge, represents a true story. While every possible effort has been made to ensure accuracy, the publisher will not assume liability for damages caused by inaccuracies in the data, and makes no warranty on the accuracy of the information contained herein. This story has not been authorized nor endorsed by Timbaland.

Contents

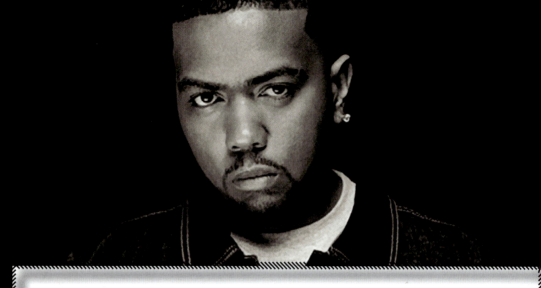

Hip-Hop lingo

Producers are the people in charge of putting together songs. A producer makes the big decisions about the music.

R&B stands for "rhythm and blues." It's a kind of music that African Americans made popular in the 1940s. It has a very strong beat. Today, it's a style of music that's a lot like hip-hop.

Pop is short for "popular." Pop music is usually light and happy, with a good beat.

Beats are the basic rhythms or pulse of a piece of music.

DJ is short for disc jockey. A DJ plays music on the radio or at a party and announces the songs.

A **drum machine** creates different types of drum sounds and also records beats to be played back later.

A **rapper** is someone who chants rhymes, often off the top of his head, sometimes with music in the background.

A **record label** is a company that produces music for singers and groups and puts out CDs.

An **album** is a group of songs collected together on a CD.

A **single** is a song that is sold by itself.

The **charts** are lists of the best-selling songs and albums for a week.

Chapter 1

Timbaland's Beginnings

Today, Timbaland is one of hip-hop's most famous **producers**. Few artists or producers have shaped the sound of hip-hop, **R&B**, or **pop** as much as Timbaland. He's been at the top of the game for more than ten years. He's had success across many types of music. For years, he's been making hits with some of the biggest names in music.

Timbaland's worked hard to get where he is today. He started making **beats** when he was just a kid, far away from the heights he's reached now.

Early Life

Timbaland's real name is Timothy Zakar Mosely. He was born on March 10, 1971. He lived in Virginia Beach, Virginia.

Tim's father was Garland Mosley. He worked for Amtrak. His mother was Latrice Mosley. Latrice ran a homeless shelter. Tim had a little brother, too. Like Tim's father, his brother was named Garland.

Growing up, there was one thing Timothy loved more than anything else. He loved music. More than any other kind of music, he loved hip-hop. From the time Tim was young, he wanted to be a **DJ**.

He loved music and wanted to make his own. He also wanted to entertain people.

When he was thirteen, Tim got his first **drum machine**. As soon as he got his hands on it, he started making beats. He even started to DJ at Virginia Beach clubs. He used the name "DJ Tiny Tim" when he performed.

Tim went to Salem High School in Virginia Beach. There, he met other young people who loved hip-hop as much as he did. Two of his friends were Terrance and Gene Thorton. The two brothers would grow up to be Pusha T and Malice from the rap group Clipse.

Tim was also friends with Melvin Barcliff. Melvin was a **rapper**. He rapped under the name Magoo. Together, Tim and Magoo started working on songs.

Another of Tim's high school friends was Missy Elliott. She'd soon be one of rap's biggest stars. Even in high school, Missy sang and rapped. She worked with an R&B group called Sista.

Then Tim met a student from another school named Pharrell Williams. Like Tim, Pharrell loved to make beats. Pharrell was in a group called The Neptunes. The Neptunes was a group of young producers.

Soon, Tim and Pharrell started their own production group. They called the group S.B.I. It stood for "Surrounded By Idiots." They started working on music together, making songs and beats.

When Tim was 17, he was working as a dishwasher in a restaurant. One of the other workers at the restaurant was always picking on him. The two didn't like each other at all. One night, as Tim was washing dishes, the other worker shot him. The bullet hit Tim in the neck and shoulder. Tim had to learn to DJ with his left hand after being shot. But it didn't keep him from following his dreams of making music.

Timbaland met Pharrell Williams when they were both in high school. The two friends started out together in the music world. Like Timbaland, Pharrell would also go on to make a big name for himself in hip-hop.

Breaking Into Music

After high school—in the early 1990s—Tim got a chance to chase his dreams of being a star DJ. He'd been working on songs with Magoo and Missy Elliott for a while. So when Missy's group Sista got the chance to go to New York to talk with a **record label**, she brought Tim and Magoo along.

The record label was called Swing Mob. DeVante Swing owned the label. He'd been a singer and producer in the R&B group Jo-

Missy Elliott is another high school friend of Timbaland's—and she too has gone on to make it big in the hip-hop world. The two friends continue to perform together, and they have each helped the other's career.

deci. Swing saw talent in Missy, Magoo, and Tim. He knew they could be something special. He signed Sista and made Missy, Magoo, and Tim part of his Swing Mob Crew.

Swing had produced lots of music. He understood how to record and how to write songs. He'd been making music with Jodeci and other artists for years. Tim wanted to learn all he could from Swing. And Swing wanted to teach everything he knew to the young DJ. Tim started working with Swing more and more to learn about being a producer.

DeVante Swing also gave Tim a new name. He called Tim "Timbaland" after Timberland boots. Now, Tim had a new name.

Early Music

Timbaland started producing some songs for DeVante Swing's group Jodeci. He also rapped on a song called "In the Meanwhile." It was the first time Timbaland had rapped on a recorded song. The song was on Jodeci's 1993 **album** *Diary of a Mad Band*.

In 1994, Timbaland also produced all the songs on Sista's album *4 All the Sistas Around da World*. The album never came out, although one **single** was released. The single, "Brand New," even hit the **charts** for a little while. Even though the album didn't come out, Timbaland's work on it still helped him get better as a producer.

The next year, Timbaland produced a song for Jodeci's album *The Show, The After-Party, The Hotel.* The song was called "Bring On Da Funk." He was also featured on the song. Also, he co-wrote a song called "Time & Place" with Jodeci for the same album.

Timbaland was living his dream. He'd gone from DJing to producing songs for a famous R&B group. DeVante Swing had given Tim the chance he needed. And he wasn't going to blow it. DeVante knew Tim had talent. But even he didn't know how far Timbaland would go.

Chapter 2

Timbaland's Road to Success

Timbaland was starting to be known for his R&B production. He left the Swing Mob crew in 1995. He'd learned a lot. By the mid 1990s, Timbaland was starting to work with more artists to make big hit songs.

Timbaland's Hits

In 1995, Timbaland started working with R&B singer Aaliyah. Tim produced nine songs for her second album. The album was called *One in a Million*. It's sold more than eight million copies around the world. Tim and Aaliyah worked very well together. They became great friends, too.

During the same year, Tim also worked with R&B singer Ginuwine. Tim worked on 12 songs for his album *Ginuwine . . . The Bachelor*. One song, "Pony," became a huge hit. It reached number six on the singles chart. It was the biggest hit Timbaland had produced so far.

Not long after that, Tim's friend Missy Elliott decided to make her first album. They had known each other for years. Now, she knew she wanted to work with Tim. Her album, called *Supa Dupa Fly*, came out

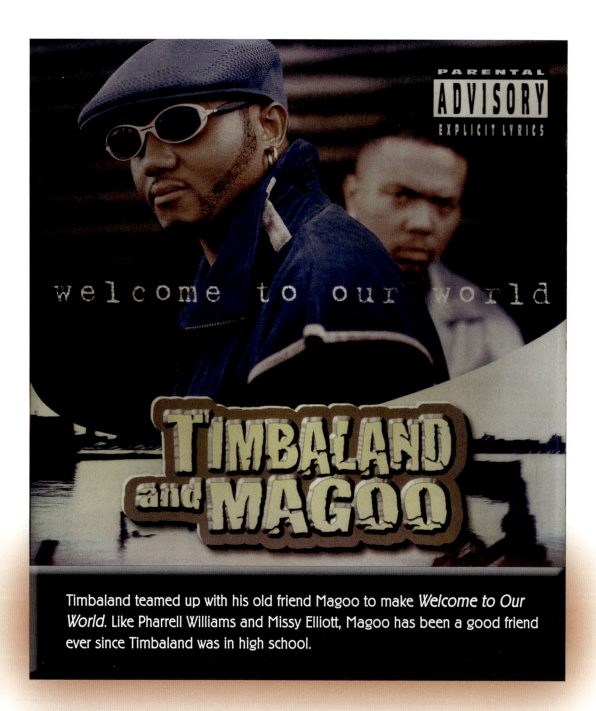

Timbaland teamed up with his old friend Magoo to make *Welcome to Our World*. Like Pharrell Williams and Missy Elliott, Magoo has been a good friend ever since Timbaland was in high school.

in 1997. The album was a hit, selling around 129,000 copies in its first week out. It went on to sell more than a million copies, too.

Next, Timbaland decided to team up with his friend Magoo. They'd been making music since they were teenagers. They got together now to make an album. They called it *Welcome to Our World*. *Welcome to Our World* came out on October 28, 1997. It was a huge hit. It sold more than a million copies in less than a year. It reached number 33 on the album charts. It also had two hit singles.

The first single was called "Up Jumps Da Boogie." The song featured Missy Elliott and Aaliyah. It made the top 20 on the singles chart. The second hit was called "Clock Strikes." It reached the top 40 on the singles chart. Tim and Magoo's friendship had produced a great album and hit songs.

Tim's Bio: Life from da Bassment

Tim loved working with other artists. He'd helped many of them make great songs and great albums. But now it was time for Timbaland to come out with an album of his own.

Timbaland's first album came out on November 24, 1998. It was called *Tim's Bio: Life from da Bassment*. Tim produced all of the songs for the album. He also rapped on many of the songs on *Tim's Bio*. Only a few of the songs didn't feature Timbaland's voice.

Tim's Bio had many guest artists. Nas, Jay-Z, Twista, and others had verses on the album. Tim's friends Missy Elliott and Magoo were also featured on it. The album was also Southern rapper Ludacris's introduction to the music world. The *Tim's Bio* song "Phat Rabbit" was the first time Ludacris had been featured on a recorded song. The song was later put out on Ludacris's first album, *Back for*

Warren Anderson Mathis (Bubba Sparxxx) grew up in the country in Georgia. He learned to love rap from New York City mixtapes his neighbor loaned him when he was in high school.

the First Time. Ginuwine and Aaliyah also helped Tim on songs for *Tim's Bio*.

Timbaland's first album was a hit. It reached number 41 on the albums chart. Tim had helped other artists be successful. His album with Magoo had sold more than a million copies. But now he'd had success with his own album. With all of his success in the 1990s, Tim started thinking about taking on bigger things.

Beat Club

It wasn't long before Timbaland wanted to start his own record label. He'd been given a chance at success in music when he was young. He wanted to make sure others had that chance, too. He wanted to share his success and help new artists.

So, Timbaland started Beat Club. Beat Club worked with Interscope Records to get music out. Tim started looking for artists for his new label. He signed Southern rapper Bubba Sparxxx to the Beat Club label. The white rapper's first album was the first album from Beat Club.

Timbaland produced seven songs for Sparxxx's first album. The album was called *Dark Days, Bright Nights*. It was a huge hit. Timbaland produced the first single, "Ugly." It was very successful. It helped the album reach number three on the album chart.

Beat Club was a success. Tim was glad to be able to help new artists. He knew how important his chance had been in his life. He wanted to help others make it, too. Beat Club was his way to give back.

Timbaland had made it to the top. He'd created hit albums and hit songs. He'd worked with some of the biggest artists in R&B and hip-hop. And now he had his own label with a hit album and popular artist. Tim's music had helped shape hip-hop and R&B. It seemed like there was nothing Timbaland couldn't do. Everything he worked on turned into a hit.

Chapter 3

Hit Maker

By the end of the 1990s, Timbaland had become one of the hottest producers in the music world. He'd paired with hip-hop and R&B greats. His songs had become hits. The albums he worked on sold well. Fans loved them.

Timbaland's sound was also becoming more and more known. People were starting to realize that Tim's songs didn't sound like anyone else's. He had his own style. And fans loved him for it! When an artist was working with Timbaland, fans knew they could look forward to something special. Tim was living his childhood dream. But soon, he'd have to deal with the loss of a great friend.

Tim Loses Aaliyah

On August 25, 2001, Aaliyah was traveling from the Bahamas to Florida. She'd been making a music video for her new song "Rock the Boat." Timbaland and Aaliyah had just finished working on her third album.

Early in the morning of the 25th, Aaliyah's plane crashed just after taking off. Aaliyah died in the crash.

Tim had worked with Aaliyah for years. He loved Aaliyah's music, and they were very good friends. Losing Aaliyah was tough for Tim. He'd helped her become one of R&B's newest stars. Now, she was gone. And she had only been 22 years old.

Aaliyah's death was a hard thing for Timbaland to face. But even though he was sad, he kept on making music.

On August 31, 2001, Tim went to Aaliyah's funeral in New York City. At the funeral, 22 doves were released into the air, one for each year Aaliyah was alive.

Tim talked to MTV about how he felt after Aaliyah died. "She was like blood, and I lost blood," he said. "Beyond the music, she was a brilliant person."

Timbaland had lost a great friend, but he wasn't going to stop making music. He and Aaliyah had always shared their love of music. Tim wanted to keep making songs that would make her proud.

Timbaland Takes Over the Music World

Timbaland came up in the 1990s, but he didn't stop making hits in the 2000s. Even losing Aaliyah couldn't slow him down.

Between 2001 and 2003, Timbaland recorded three albums with Missy Elliott. The first was called *Miss E . . . So Addictive* and came out in 2001. The song "Get Ur Freak On" was a huge hit from the album. The next album was called *Under Construction*. Timbaland produced the hit song "Work It" for *Under Construction*. In 2003, Tim and Missy paired up again for *This Is Not a Test!*

Timbaland also worked with Ludacris again. Tim and Luda had recorded "Phat Rabbit" together in the late '90s. Now, in 2001, Timbaland produced Ludacris's first album, *Rollout (My Business)*. They included "Phat Rabbit" on this album, too. *Rollout* was a big hit for Ludacris. It helped him get new fans and sell albums.

Timbaland also started working with Jay-Z in 2001 and 2002. Tim produced "Hola Hovito" for Jay's *The Blueprint*. The next year, the two worked on three songs for *The Blueprint 2*.

In 2002, Justin Timberlake was looking for producers to work on his first solo album. Timberlake turned to Timbaland to help him make a new sound. Timbaland produced four songs for Timberlake's album *Justified*. One of the songs was the hit "Cry Me a River."

During the early 2000s, Timbaland and Magoo also teamed up for another two albums. Their second album was called *Indecent Proposal*. The album came out on November 20, 2001. It wasn't as big a hit as their first. Still, it made it to number 29 on the album charts. Their third album, *Under Construction, Part II*, was released in 2003.

Tim was working with some of music's biggest stars. In the early 2000s, artists knew that working with Timbaland meant getting good music. His beats had become famous. The songs he worked on became hits.

Timbaland Meets Danja

In 2001, Timbaland met a young producer named Nate "Danja" Hills. It was a meeting that would end in the two producers working together for years. Danja had grown up in Virginia Beach, Virginia, just like Tim. His real name was Floyd Nathanial Hills.

When he was a teenager, Danja started to play drums and piano. Soon, he was making his own songs and beats. When he grew up, he became a music producer. In 2000, he worked on R&B group Blackstreet's album *Level II*. A year later, he met Timbaland and played him some of his music. And just two years after that, Tim and Danja were working together.

Tim taught Danja a lot about how to make hit songs. The two producers became friends. They worked well together. They worked on music for many different artists. They worked on songs for Nelly Furtado, Justin Timberlake, and rappers like The Game and Lloyd Banks.

Timbaland was still going strong. He was still making hits with some of the biggest artists in the music world. But his successes

Timbaland's friends have always helped him grow. His new friend Danja would help his career in lots of ways. And Danja learned a lot from Timbaland as well.

Timbaland and Timberlake together!

didn't come without new problems and hardships. He'd lost one of his best friends when Aaliyah died. His Beat Club label was also having hard times. It wasn't long before the label closed down.

Timbaland was still one of the biggest producers in hip-hop and R&B. And by working with artists like Justin Timberlake, he'd shown he could make great pop music, too. Tim wasn't going to stop making music. He wasn't going to give up when things got hard. Tim just kept on doing what he did best—making great music.

Hip-Hop lingo

Each year, the National Academy of Recording Arts and Sciences gives out the **Grammy Awards** (short for Gramophone Awards)– or Grammys–to people who have done something really big in the music industry.

When someone has been **nominated**, he has been picked as one of the people who might win an award.

A **collaboration** is when two or more people work together on a project.

Chapter 4

Shock to the System

By the mid 2000s, Timbaland had become one of hip-hop's most famous producers. He was making hits with many artists. Tim helped shape the sound of hip-hop. But he was also changing the sound of pop music. Tim's songs had become so popular that artists outside of hip-hop wanted to work with him. His sound was very well known. He'd brought his own style to people around the world. And they only wanted more.

Mosely Music Group

Timbaland's Beat Club Records didn't work out. The company wasn't as successful as Tim wanted it to be. But he still wanted to run his own label. He knew he could be successful with his own company. He just needed to try again.

In 2006, Timbaland started another record label. He called the new company Mosely Music Group. Timbaland brought some of the artists he worked with on Beat Club Records. Singer Nelly Furtado came to Mosely Music Group. So did R&B singer Keri Hilson. Rapper D.O.E. was also on Tim's new label. New band OneRepublic signed to Mosley Music Group, too.

The first album Mosley Music Group put out was Nelly Furtado's *Loose*. The label also put out OneRepublic's first album. It was called *Dreaming Out Loud*. The albums were both big hits. They helped Mosely Music Group succeed.

Shock Value

Timbaland put out an album of his own with his new label, too. He called the album *Timbaland Presents Shock Value*. It came out on April 3, 2007.

Shock Value featured many guest artists working with Tim. 50 Cent, Nelly Furtado, Missy Elliot, and Dr. Dre all worked on songs for the album. On *Shock Value*, Tim worked with lots of artists fans might not have expected. For example, Elton John and the rock band Fall Out Boy helped out on songs for the album.

The first single from *Shock Value* was called "Give It to Me." The song featured Nelly Furtado and Justin Timberlake. It was released on February 6, 2007. The song was a big hit. It reached number one on the singles chart in the United States. It also reached the top of the charts in the UK.

"Give It to Me" was Timbaland's first number-one song on his own. He'd had lots of hits before, but usually as a producer only. Now, he was making hits for himself and getting the credit for them.

The second single from *Shock Value* was called "The Way I Are." Singer Keri Hilson sang the song's chorus. The song also featured rapper D.O.E. Both Hilson and D.O.E. were part of Timbaland's Mosely Music Group. The song was released on July 9, 2007. It was an even bigger hit than "Give It to Me." The song reached the number-one spot on charts around the world. It was a number-one song in Ireland, Australia, Norway, and the UK "The Way I Are"

Timbaland wasn't afraid to stretch his creative boundary lines. He even worked with Elton John, a musician who at first glance doesn't seem to have a lot in common with Timbaland!

Busta Rhymes was one of the rappers for whom Timbaland produced songs.

made it to number three on the U.S. singles chart. The single sold more than two million copies in the United States.

The third single was called "Throw It on Me." It was released July 23, 2007. Timbaland worked on the song with the rock band The Hives. The song made it onto the charts in Australia, but wasn't a hit in the same way the other singles had been.

The fourth single from *Shock Value* was a remix of OneRepublic's "Apologize." It came out on September 17, 2007. The song had first come out on OneRepublic's first album. Tim's remix of "Apologize" was a huge hit. The song made it to number two on the U.S. singles chart. It sold more than three million copies in the United States, too. The song was a giant hit all around the world. It reached number one on singles charts in Australia, Germany, Italy, Sweden, and Canada.

The last single from *Shock Value* was called "Scream." The song came out as a single on December 11, 2007. Keri Hilson sang on the song. So did Nicole Scherzinger of the Pussycat Dolls. "Scream" wasn't as big a hit as some of *Shock Value*'s other singles. But it was still very successful. The song made it onto singles charts in Europe, Canada, and Australia.

Shock Value was a giant hit for Timbaland. The album had many hit singles and sold well. In its first week out it sold 138,000 copies. In that first week, it came in at number five on the albums chart in the United States. *Shock Value* also reached number two on the charts in the UK. Since its release, *Shock Value* has sold more than two million copies around the world.

The years 2006 and 2007 were big ones for Timbaland. He'd made hits with other artists. He'd had hits of his own. He also worked with some of music's biggest stars.

In 2006, Timbaland produced songs for Busta Rhymes and Snoop Dogg. He worked on songs for Omarion and Young Jeezy.

Tim also helped make most of the songs for two big albums in 2006. He produced almost every song on Justin Timberlake's *FutureSex/LoveSounds* and Nelly Furtado's *Loose*. Tim worked well with both Timberlake and Furtado. The two albums were huge hits.

Timbaland worked with some of the biggest names in hip-hop, including Kanye West.

In 2007, not only did Tim put out *Shock Value*, but he also worked on lots of songs with other artists. He worked with singer Björk, rapper M.I.A., 50 Cent, Kanye West, and Rihanna.

After *Shock Value* and all the songs Tim worked on between 2006 and 2007, he was one of the biggest producers around. Tim had been making hits for more than ten years. Everyone wanted to work with him. No matter what kind of music, whether R&B, rap, rock, or pop, Timbaland could bring out a new side of an artist. He'd also finally made his own second album with *Shock Value*. Tim's fans couldn't have been happier.

2008 Grammys

At the 2008 **Grammy Awards**, Timbaland was **nominated** for five awards. He was up for Best Rap Song for "Ayo Technology," a song he'd done with 50 Cent and Justin Timberlake. His work on Justin Timberlake's 2007 album also brought Tim two nominations. "LoveStoned/I Think She Knows" was up for Best Dance Recording. "What Goes Around . . . Comes Around" was up for Record of the Year.

Timbaland was also nominated for his own song, "Give It to Me." The song was up for Best Pop **Collaboration** with Vocals. Tim was even nominated for Producer of the Year (Non-classical).

Tim won one award on February 10, 2008, the night of the Grammys. He and Justin Timberlake won Best Dance Recording for "LoveStoned/I Think She Knows." But even though he didn't win every Grammy he was up for, he was still on top of the music world.

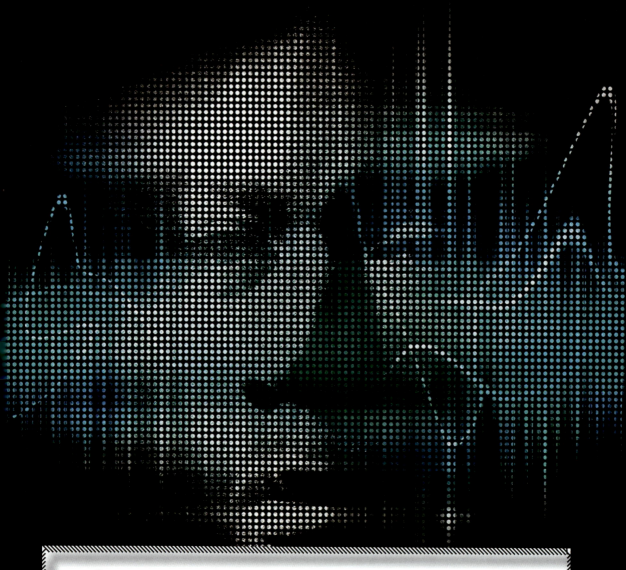

TIMBALAND
PRESENTS

Hip-Hop lingo
Tracks are parts—usually songs—of an album.

SHOCK VALUE II

Chapter 5

Timbaland on Top

With his *Shock Value* album, Timbaland proved he was not just another great producer. The album sold millions of copies. The singles were hits. Timbaland had made hits with other artists. Now, his own album was a hit. He'd gone from making **tracks** for other artists, to making his own music, pulling in others when he wanted to. Timbaland was on top of the music world.

Shock Value II

Timbaland put out *Shock Value II* on December 4, 2009. Like the first *Shock Value*, the album had lots of guest artists. Justin Timberlake, JoJo, Drake, Katy Perry, Miley Cyrus, and Daughtry all helped on songs for the album. The album also featured Jet, OneRepublic, Keri Hilson, and The Fray.

The first single from the new *Shock Value* was called "Morning After Dark." The song featured Nelly Furtado and French singer SoShy. It was released as a single on October 26, 2009. The song did well around the world. It wasn't as big a hit as some of the songs from the first *Shock Value*. But it was still a hit. The song made it into the top 10 on singles charts in the UK, Germany, Sweden, and Belgium. It reached the top 20 in Australia, Ireland, Norway, Denmark, and other European countries.

Shock Value II's second single was called "Say Something." The song featured Canadian rapper Drake. "Say Something" came out as a single on November 3, 2009. The song was a hit. It reached number 23 on the Hot 100 singles chart.

Timbaland featured a song by Katy Perry on his new album—and people all over the world loved it!

The third single from the album was called "Carry Out." The song featured Tim's friend Justin Timberlake. The two had had a lot of success working on the first *Shock Value* and Timberlake's 2006 album. "Carry Out" came out on December 1, 2009. The song became the biggest hit from *Shock Value II.* It reached the top 10 on singles charts around the world. "Carry Out" made it to number six on the UK singles chart. In Canada, it reached number seven. In Ireland, it reached number three. In the United States, the song made it to number 11 on the singles chart. "Carry Out" was another huge success for Timbaland and Justin Timberlake.

The last single from *Shock Value II* was called "If We Ever Meet Again." The song featured singer Katy Perry. It came out on February 15, 2010. The song was a hit all over the world. It reached the top 10 on singles charts in Spain, the UK, Canada, Australia, Switzerland, and many others. In the United States, the song made it to number 37 on the singles chart.

Shock Value II wasn't as big a hit as the first *Shock Value*. In its first week out, it sold just over 37,000 copies. Slow sales for one album weren't going to stop Timbaland from making more music, though. He told fans that *Shock Value III* would come out in 2011.

Timbaland Thursdays

In August 2010, rapper Kanye West started G.O.O.D. Fridays. Kanye put out a new song every Friday on his website. G.O.O.D. Fridays was a big hit with fans. They loved being able to hear new songs each week. It helped Kanye get out the word about his new album. It also helped him connect with his fans. Lots of rappers had put out their music for free online. But no one as famous as Kanye had tried giving their music away over the Internet.

G.O.O.D. Fridays was such a hit with fans that other artists wanted to try the same thing. Producer Swizz Beatz said he'd start giving away music on his own website. He began Monster Mondays in October 2010. Snoop Dogg started putting out new music for free as well. Soon, Timbaland wanted to try it, too.

In November 2010, Timbaland announced Timbo Thursday. Tim would put out new songs on Thursdays. In January 2011, Tim put out the first song for Timbo Thursday. On January 13, he released one of his new songs featuring Missy Elliott. One Timbo Thursday song, "Lil Apartment," was released on January 27. The song featured rappers Attitude and Six2. "Lil Apartment" was meant to be on the first *Shock Value*. Instead, Timbaland put it out for free online. Timbaland kept Timbo Thursdays going for months. He didn't stop giving away new, free music until he had to go work on other artists' music.

Timbo Thursday gave Tim a way to get new music to his fans as fast as he could. It was a way for him to connect to the people who loved his music. It was also a great way to remind people that Timbaland was still on top of his game.

Always Believing Foundation

Timbaland has had a lot of success in music. He's done things most people can only dream about. With all his success, Tim knows it's important to give back. He's been able to reach his dreams. Now that he has, he understands that he can help others reach theirs.

Tim started the Always Believing Foundation in 2008. He wanted Always Believing to help teach kids how to fight obesity. Obesity means weighing more than is healthy. Tim understands that childhood obesity is a major problem in the United States.

Timbaland believes music can play a big role in getting kids fit. He wants kids to learn about how to stay active and stay healthy. With Always Believing, Tim wants to teach kids about eating right and exercising.

Timbaland believes that along with his success comes the responsibility to help others.

There's only one Timbaland!

Giving back is a big part of Timbaland's life. He knows how important it is to share success with others. Through his music and the Always Believing Foundation, Tim wants to make the world a better place.

Looking to the Future

Timbaland is one of the biggest producers working in music today. Few producers can imagine having as much success as Tim. He's worked for almost 20 years making music. He's produced songs for some of the greatest hip-hop and pop artists of all time.

He's also put out his own hit albums. In 2011, he told fans that *Shock Value III* would be released in 2012. The album's first single, "Pass At Me," came out in September 2011.

Tim's sound has helped shape pop, hip-hop, and dance music. When a song Timbaland worked on comes on the radio or in the club, you can tell it's his. His beats are fresh and fun. They sound different from other producers. Tim's sound is all his own. Many try to sound like him, but there's only one Timbaland. And he's still working on more new music all the time.

1971   Timothy Zachery Mosley (also known as "Timbaland") is born on March 10, in Virginia.

1970s   Timothy begins making hip-hop backing tracks on his Casio keyboard.

1985   Timothy starts classes at Salem High School. It is here that he meets rapper Melvn Barcliff, also known as Magoo.

1986   When he is 15 years old, Timothy is shot. He spends nine months in bed. During this time, he learns how to deejay using his left hand.

1995   Timothy gets his first big break when DeVante Swing asks him to produce his album *The Show*. It is DeVante Swing who gives Timothy the nickname "Timbaland," after his Timberland boots.

1997   Timbaland and Magoo release their first album, *Welcome to Our World*.

1998   Timbaland releases his first solo album, *Tim's Bio: Life from da Bassment*

2001   Timbaland and Magoo's second album is released, called *Indecent Proposal.*

One of his best friends, Aaliyah, dies in a plane crash.

He produces the Bubba Sparxxx album *Dark Days, Bright Nights.*

2003   Timbaland and Magoo's third album is released, called *Under Construction, Part II.*

He works on Justin Timberlake's first solo album, *Justified*. The album is a huge success and brings Timbaland a lot of attention.

2007   Timbaland releases a solo album called *Shock Value*. The album features many big name artists, including 50 Cent, Dr. Dre, Elton John, Nelly Furtado, and Missy Elliott.

BET gives him the Producer of the Year award.

He wins a Grammy Award for Best Dance Recording ("Sexyback.")

2008   Timbaland becomes the first official producer for Verizon Wireless.

He produces tracks for Chris Cornell, Ashlee Simpson, The Pussycat Dolls, Bust Rhymes, Flo Rida, and Lindsay Lohan.

He is given the Songwriter of the Year award.

He wins a Grammy Award for Best Dance Recording ("Lovestoned/I Think She Knows.")

2009   He releases *Shock Value II*.

2010   He continues to produce albums for big name artists, including The Game and Missy Elliott.

Timbaland begins giving away music online as part of Timbo Thursday.

2011   Timbaland releases "Pass At Me," the first single from *Shock Value III*.

In Books

Baker, Soren. *The History of Rap and Hip Hop*. San Diego, Calif.: Lucent, 2006.

Comissiong, Solomon W. F. *How Jamal Discovered Hip-Hop Culture*. New York: Xlibris, 2008.

Cornish, Melanie. *The History of Hip Hop*. New York: Crabtree, 2009.

Czekaj, Jef. *Hip and Hop, Don't Stop!* New York: Hyperion, 2010.

Haskins, Jim. *One Nation Under a Groove: Rap Music and Its Roots*. New York: Jump at the Sun, 2000.

Hatch, Thomas. *A History of Hip-Hop: The Roots of Rap*. Portsmouth, N.H.: Red Bricklearning, 2005.

Websites

Hip Hop Music Production
www.hiphopproduction.com

Official Site
www.timbalandmusic.com

Timbaland on IMDB
www.imdb.com/name/nm0608856

Timbaland on MTV
www.mtv.com/music/artist/timbaland/artist.jhtml

Timbaland on MySpace
www.myspace.com/timbaland

Discography

Albums

1998   Tim's Bio: Life from da Bassment

2007   Shock Value

2009   Shock Value II

Index

About the Author

C.F. Earl is a writer living and working in Binghamton, New York. Earl writes mostly on social and historical topics, including health, the military, and finances. An avid student of the world around him, and particularly fascinated with almost any current issue, C.F. Earl hopes to continue to write for books, websites, and other publications for as long as he is able.

Picture Credits